Cat Horoscopes

& Other Diversions

Cat Horoscopes

& Other Diversions

Laissez les bon
temps rouler!

Dan Borengasser

Dan Borengasser

SpringStreet Books
Philadelphia

SpringStreet Books
PO Box 1042
Philadelphia, PA 19105

Printed in the United States of America
ISBN 978-0-9795204-1-9

This book is printed on acid-free paper.

Contents

Cat Horoscopes

CATS ARE, of course, one of the most popular pets. However, to properly care for a cat, you must understand the feline personality. This isn't easy since cats aren't exactly what you'd call "chummy."

To help you better appreciate your kitty, I've consulted the stars, the sun, the moon and a one-eyed mystic from Oshkosh known as Swami River. From this research, I've compiled a comprehensive cat horoscope:

ARIES (March 21–April 19): The Aries cat is sneaky, impulsive and loves to eat June bugs. Often shy and retiring, the Aries feline can hide under the sofa for weeks, coming out only occasionally to vomit.

TAURUS (April 20–May 20): The Taurus cat is bull-headed and sneaky. You'll know the Taurus cat by its refusal to respond to any name except "Kitty." Its idea of affection is rubbing up against your ankles. If this causes you to trip, the Taurus cat will purr with contentment.

GEMINI (May 21–June 20): The sign of the twins, the Gemini cat has a dual personality, one aloof and sneaky, the other haughty and sneaky. Gemini cats are athletic. They exercise by climbing the drapes, leaping up on the kitchen counter or slinging suspicious clumps of kitty litter all over the floor.

CANCER (June 21–July 22): The Cancer cat is crabby. Also known to be sullen, sneaky and spoiled, this cat expects to have the complete run of the house. Garfield is a Cancer.

LEO (July 23–August 22): The Leo cat, sneaky, independent and finicky, will only eat the most expensive cat food on the market. It would starve before eating dry cat food. This cat finds great pleasure in knocking expensive things off of tables.

VIRGO (August 23–September 22): Most Virgo cats are black. They enjoy the occult, black magic and causing bad luck for humans. They are incredibly sneaky.

LIBRA (September 23–October 22): The Libra cat is self-absorbed, sneaky and loves to torment baby birds. The Libra kitty is remarkable in that it only has eight lives, three of which are thoroughly worthless.

SCORPIO (October 23–November 21): Don't even think of getting a Scorpio cat. All Scorpio cats are psychotic. And, of course, sneaky.

SAGITTARIUS (November 22–December 21): Born under the sign of the hairball, Sagittarius cats spend every waking moment giving themselves tongue baths. The Sagittarius cat is the least sneaky of all the signs.

CAPRICORN (December 22–January 19):
Capricorn cats are extraordinarily curious, often
the victims of a fatal accident because of this
quality. They enjoy jumping on you as you're
taking a nap and then batting your nose with their
claws. Capricorn cats are noted for their amazing
sneakiness.

AQUARIUS (January 20–February 18): Aquarius
is the water sign. All cats hate water. Therefore, no
cats are ever born during this time.

PISCES (February 19–March 20): There's
something fishy about cats born under the sign of
Pisces. I guess you could say they're sneaky.

As you can see from the horoscope, each sign
has its good points and its bad points.

How do you choose? Which is the best cat for
you?

It's hard to say, but from my experience, the
perfect cat is one whose sun is in Sagittarius,
whose moon is in Aries and whose house is across
town.

The Psychic Hotline

PSYCHIC HOTLINES. Who came up with that?

You pay some exorbitant phone charge and get advice from a stranger who claims to know your past, present and future. First of all, I already know my past and present, so why do I need someone to tell me about them? Besides, there are some moments I'd just as soon forget.

And the future? Well, there's the trick—no way to know if the psychic's right or wrong. With most things you buy, if you're not completely satisfied, you can take it back. Also, a new toaster or TV or car comes with a warranty. But not your future, pal. The guy on the other end of the phone can tell you that you're going to quit your job and run out on your family to travel the country as a snake charmer, and you're still going to be coughing up good money to hear this.

But then I realize that if the general public will give phone psychics mucho bucks a minute, they'll give money to anybody.

Even me.

I decide to open my own psychic hotline, charge two dollars a minute and run my competitors out of town.

Over the next week, I have an extra phone installed and run an ad in a supermarket tabloid. I'm ready for business.

The phone rings.

My first customer.

"Discount Psychic Hotline," I answer. "We knew you'd call. Would you like to speak to a warlock, a witch, a tarot card reader, a palmist or Elvis?"

There is a pause, and a man cautiously replies, "A witch."

"Witch Borengasser speaking," I reply.

"You're a witch? I thought witches were female."

"I've got a cold. What can I do for you?"

"Can you cast a spell?"

"Sorry. My liability insurance doesn't cover casting spells. How about some nice aspersions? I can cast aspersions."

"No, thanks. Ahh ... what exactly can you do?"

"I can tell your fortune by reading okra."

"What? Why would anyone read okra?"

"Why not? What else can you do with okra? Okay, I'm examining an okra pod. You must concentrate. Let's see. It's coming through now. You are intelligent, have a great personality, have many hidden talents and are often misunderstood by those around you."

"Wow. That's exactly right. How did you know that?"

"Hey, what can I tell you? I'm a witch. Call again."

The phone rings.

"Discount Psychic Hotline. We knew you'd call. Would you like to speak to a warlock, a witch, a tarot card reader, a palmist or Elvis?"

"Ahh … a palmist."

"Palmist Borengasser speaking."

"Don't you have to see my hand to read my palm?"

"Aren't you holding the phone in the palm of your hand?"

"Well, yes."

"Close enough. How can I help you?"

"What can you tell me about my finances?"

"You will soon spend some money foolishly."

"When?"

"Right now. Thanks for calling."

The phone rings.

"Discount Psychic Hotline. We knew you'd call. Would you like to speak to a warlock, a witch, a tarot card reader, a palmist or Elvis?"

"How about Elvis?" a woman's voice requests.

"Elvis speaking."

"You don't sound like Elvis."

"Give me a break. I haven't exactly been the picture of health. What would you like to know?"

"What's the future hold for me?"

"I see a man in your life."

"What's he like?"

"A hunka, hunka burning love. Thanks for calling."

The phone rings.

"Discount Psychic Hotline. We knew you'd call. Would you like to speak to a warlock, a witch, a tarot card reader, a palmist or Elvis?"

"Let me speak to your accounting department."

I get an uneasy feeling. "Who may I say is calling?"

"The IRS."

As I quickly hang up, I realize that I'll soon be out of the psychic hotline business.

Some futures you can figure out without a fortuneteller.

Cleaning the Garage

THIS IS the universal Rule of Garages—your possessions will automatically accumulate to fill all available garage space. (Note: In garage language, "possessions" means "junk.")

It doesn't make any difference if you have a one-car or a ten-car garage. You'll fill it up.

Fact: Most people still have unopened boxes in their garage from their last move.

Fact: Most people have things in their garage older than they are, most of which they are totally unaware, possibly some pre-Columbian artifacts or a piece of flatware from the original thirteen colonies.

Usually, I try not to look in our garage. I quickly park the car and enter the house, averting my eyes from the inscrutable stacks of odds and ends.

But at the lovely Mrs. Borengasser's urging (and, wow, can the lovely Mrs. Borengasser urge!), I decide to take on the Herculean task of cleaning the garage.

And today's the day.

Screwing up my courage, I step through the door and survey the scene

It's like entering another world, a scene from an old Vincent Price movie. Even during the day, the garage is dim. Dark, dusty shapes line the walls. There are dozens of shelves, some filled with misshapen cartons, some with old tools, some with strange, unrecognizable items. The empty eye sockets of my skull collection stare down at me, mocking. Almost everything is covered with a coating of spider webs and cat hair.

I feel thousands of eyes on me. My every move is being watched. Many of those spying on me are spiders. But there are others—insects, reptiles, rodents, perhaps a few larger mammals, possibly even a primate or two. Who's to say? Anything could be lurking in the corners and cubbyholes.

There's no doubt about it. I'm in a hostile environment. These critters know I'm up to no good.

But I begin.

Hour One: I kill several hundred spiders, but it isn't easy. In a rare example of inter-species cooperation, several different types of spiders have banded together to try and encase me in a giant web. I defeat them, but the encounter weakens my resolve. Nevertheless, in a dazzling display of cleaning fervor, I decide to get rid of the fencing foil that I haven't used in a quarter century.

Hour Two: I discover several ancient boxes that I don't recognize. One says "Pandora's Stuff – Keep Out!" I decide it might be better to leave it unopened. Another carton is labeled "Old Shoes." Still another, "Broken China." I don't feel courageous enough to open these either, but I do dust them off and move them around a little.

Hour Three: Nothing much gets accomplished during hour three because I'm lured into reading "Life in These United States" humor pieces in a box of old *Reader's Digests*.

Hour Four: I find that I've begun saying, "You never know when these will come in handy." It makes no difference to what I'm referring— tomato stakes, paper bags or pieces of string. And I'm right. They could come in handy. But this attitude definitely hinders any massive purging. To maintain my self-respect, I throw out a large box labeled "Oily Rags."

I've finally finished.

Don't get me wrong. The job's not done. I'm just finished.

Oh, I know there are people out there with immaculate garages, with a place for everything and everything in its place, with tools all hanging daintily from hooks on pegboard. Maybe the pegboard even has the outline of each particular tool. And, of course, the floors have no oil spots.

But I'm not one of those people.

To be truthful, I don't really trust someone with a neat garage. In fact, show me a man with a neat garage and I'll show you someone who classifies and pigeonholes and categorizes. Everything has to be labeled and filed away.

When this guy meets you, he'll do to you what he did to his garage. He'll try to sort you out and label you. To him, you're not a unique combination of talents and shortcomings, likes and dislikes, all blended together in a rich, diverse personality. Instead, he'll see you as a bleeding heart liberal or a yellow dog Democrat or a dyed-in-the-wool Republican or a dumb redneck.

And if you feel that you yourself have a tendency to be judgmental and to label people, it's not too late to do something about it. Stop cleaning your garage!

Dieting

FOR MANY, dieting is a way of life.

If you're wondering whether you, too, should be on a diet, here are several telltale signs:

Do you have to ask someone whether your shoes are tied?

When you recently tried on last year's swimsuit, did you have to be extricated from it with the Jaws of Life?

Does the Pillsbury Doughboy have a better physique?

When you wear that old sweatshirt, does it look like Spandex?

When you refer to your chin, do you use the plural?

Do you have wattles?

Perhaps you're already on a diet. Then, the question to ask yourself is whether you feel reasonably happy and well adjusted. If the answer is yes, then most likely your diet is a bad one. For a diet to be effective, you should be miserable. Remember that the first three letters of "diet" spell "die."

I've been on a diet for decades. Over the years,

I've lost four and a half tons. Unfortunately, during that time, I've also gained 9,010 pounds, which means I still need to lose ten more.

Along the way, I've learned some valuable lessons about dieting, nutrition and waist management:

1. The number one most fattening substance is food. Ask anyone concerned about his/her weight and he/she will tell you the culprit was food.

2. All food is fattening. It merely depends on the volume. A stick of celery may not do much damage. But sit down to a meal of four thousand stalks and you're going to gain weight.

3. Never take money into a supermarket. Supermarkets are loaded with food. And, as you'll recall from above, food is fattening.

4. The most effective diet is the Flu Diet. And it's the easiest. Simply catch the flu. You'll lose ten pounds the first week. (Warning: If this diet lasts longer than six months, you may actually be on the more troublesome Dysentery Diet.)

5. A truly amazing diet is the Hocolate Diet. It's simple. Never eat anything that ends in the letters h-o-c-o-l-a-t-e. I don't know how or why this works, but somehow it does.

6. Don't count on the old advice that you should watch what you eat. I watched what I ate for years. In fact, I watched it till it disappeared into my mouth. I didn't lose a milligram.

7. Don't weigh yourself everyday. In fact, I recommend throwing away your scales. After all, a scale is giving you only one machine's opinion. And, as you know, a dollar ninety-five and an opinion will buy you a cup of coffee. (Hold the cream and sugar.)

8. Don't think of your weight in numbers. Numbers are depressing. If you're ten pounds overweight, tell people you're "big-boned." Twenty pounds, "pleasingly plump." Thirty pounds, "corn fed."

9. Exercise. Small lifestyle changes can make a big difference. Chew your food more vigorously. Several times a day, engage in power-blinking. (Warning: If you experience any discomfort, consult a physician.) Get rid of the TV remote control. Instead of driving to the end of the driveway to get the paper, walk.

One out of every three Americans is obese. This is a frightening fact. But there are two ways you can avoid being a victim of this statistic. Number one, change nationalities. Number two, always travel with two other Americans, one of whom is obese. Then you don't even need to be on a diet.

Bon appétit.

Income Tax

THE DEADLINE for submitting your income tax is approaching. (The great thing about this statement is that it's always true.)

The general rule of taxes is that, if you're getting a refund, file immediately. If you owe money, stall.

To help you with your taxes, I've provided answers to some commonly asked questions.

Question: What exactly is a tax shelter?

Answer: A tax shelter is a place to hide where the IRS can't find you. It is also referred to as a tax "hidey-hole." You've probably heard that this year there are fewer tax shelters. This is true, although there are still a few good ones in northern Idaho and the Dakotas.

Question: Who are considered legal dependents?

Answer: This should be obvious. Dependents are those who depend on you. Thus, your mate, your children, your dog, your parakeet, your guppies, your boss and your no-good Uncle Hershel can all be considered dependents.

Question: What deductions are acceptable?

Answer: These change from year to year and often seem quite arbitrary. As an example, among the items you can legally deduct this year are dependents, mortgage interest, Lite beer, Lotto tickets and specially marked packages of Cap'n Crunch.

Question: Are tax laws different this year from the previous year?

Answer: Yes, indeed. They change every year. And you'll be surprised to find out that they're more complicated this year. Some legislators are concerned that the tax laws are reaching the point where they can't become any more complicated. Since hundreds of thousands of jobs depend on the tax forms being incomprehensible, this is a crisis in the making. One approach being discussed is to base the tax computations on trigonometry instead of common arithmetic. For instance, the only way you can receive a refund is if your cosine is greater than or equal to the square of your hypotenuse. Another committee is recommending that the tax laws be tied in with the Unified Wave Theory.

Question: What is a flat tax? Isn't it supposed to make paying taxes simpler?

Answer: You must have skipped over the previous answer. Nothing will ever make paying taxes simpler. *Nothing. Ever.* In fact, one of the constitutional amendments, twenty-eight or twenty-nine, expressly forbids having simple tax laws. The flat tax actually started as a joke the Secretary of the Treasury made at a cocktail party.

Question: Didn't I read that the IRS eliminated routine audits several years ago?

Answer: Yes, although there are still some situations that automatically raise a red flag for tax auditors, for instance, if you are a member of organized crime or if you have previously served time for tax fraud.

Question: Does this mean that my chances of being audited are slim?

Answer: No, not really. Actually, you and your financial records are always being watched, even at this very second, just in case you happen to develop some crazy political or socioeconomic ideas and have to be permanently put away. A small price to pay for democracy.

Question: Doesn't it seem as if much of our tax money is wasted or spent foolishly, like on a $3.7 million pith helmet or a billion dollar toilet seat?

Answer: Hey, pal, who are you to criticize? Haven't you ever gone out and blown a few bucks? Thousands of people watch pay-per-view wrestling, and you were probably one of them, so you can climb down off your high horse.

Question: I didn't do the pay-per-view wrestling thing, but I once bought a Slim-a-nizer after watching a television infomercial.

Answer: Exactly. See what I mean?

Question: The IRS often seems so hostile and combative that I'm completely intimidated. Is this normal?

Answer: Absolutely, but the IRS is trying to change their image. For example, next year, everyone who has to mail in a check will receive a complimentary flower.

Question: Really? That's nice. What kind of flower?

Answer: It's called the yellow rose of taxes.

Future Air Travel

IT'S A DAY in some not-too-distant future.

I'm getting ready to take an airplane to New York.

Domestic air travel has changed over the last few years. Safety concerns and low profitability have significantly altered the way airlines do business.

One of the latest regulations is the thirty-seven page flight request that I had to file three weeks before my scheduled departure. In it, I had to list my travel itinerary, the exact contents of my luggage and my family tree back to the year 1700. One loony cousin and my departure could have been delayed for months.

But my trip has been preliminarily approved, and I set out for the airport.

Of course, I have to arrive four hours in advance for my pre-flight evaluation. Entering the airport, I step up to the airline counter.

"Good morning, sir," a polite young man named Carl greets me. "What is your final destination today?"

"New York," I reply.

"Fine, may I see eleven forms of identification, five with your photo, two with your fingerprints and one with your DNA profile?"

I give him what he requests.

"And did you bring a notary public to verify these IDs, sir?"

"Yes, this is Herman the Notary. Herman, this is Carl the Travel Attendant." Herman quickly verifies my identification, I pay him and he leaves.

"Okay, now I have to ask you several questions, sir." He holds out a Bible, and I place my hand on it. "Do you solemnly swear to tell the truth, the whole truth and nothing but the truth?" Carl asks.

"I do."

"Have you touched anyone else's luggage or allowed anyone to touch yours over the last seven days?"

"No."

"In the last two weeks, have you socialized with any drug lords?"

"No."

"Have you ever smoked a Cuban cigar?"

"Certainly not."

"Fine, now if you'll just step into this room, we'll take care of your personal exam."

I do as he says. As usual, the strip search is efficient and unbelievably humiliating. While I'm standing there, a team of bloodhounds snorts through all my clothing and, other than a five-week-old pizza stain, they find nothing. Then I have to lie down on a floor mat so the dogs can sniff me. And other than the shock of seven cold, wet canine noses poking and prodding, this exam goes smoothly.

The x-ray is another matter. The technician glares suspiciously at me. "What's this?" he demands, pointing at my x-ray. "A kidney-shaped weapon?"

"Uh … actually, it is a kidney," I assure him. "My kidney."

He looks closer. "Oh, so it is. We can't be too careful, you know."

Even though I've just been x-rayed and strip searched, I still have to go through the metal detector. I think the Federal Aviation Administration maintains them out of a sense of nostalgia. Nevertheless, metal detectors are a lot more sensitive these days. I have to have my zipper replaced with Velcro and pry three old fillings off my teeth.

Next, I'm escorted into a small room for my MRI. Everything passes muster, although the technician does advise me that my lower back looks a little out of alignment.

Finally, Carl approaches me. "Congratulations, sir. You have qualified for the flight to New York," he says, handing me my luggage receipts and a pre-flight diploma.

Not a moment too soon. I've been steadily losing my patience through this exasperating process. One more aggravation and I'm going to blow like Mount Vesuvius.

"Fine," I respond through gritted teeth. "Are you serving any food on this flight?"

"Yes, indeed, sir. This is a snack flight. As soon as we reach our cruising altitude, the flight attendant will be giving everyone a sip of water, a pistachio nut and a breath mint."

"Yummy," I snarl.

As I start to turn away, Carl adds, "By the way, sir, this has been designated a childless flight."

I turn back to face him. "A childless flight?" I ask, amazed. "No children are allowed?"

"No, sir. None."

Suddenly, everything is worth it.

Online Romance

AN INCREASINGLY popular place for seeking romance is the Internet.

Of course, wherever there's romance, there's misunderstanding, insecurity and heartache. And wherever there's misunderstanding, insecurity and heartache, there's the need for expert advice on relationships. Therefore, I decide to become Dr. Cyberlove, online advisor for the lovelorn.

In no time, I'm receiving questions from the love smitten and romantically miserable.

♦ ♦ ♦

Dear Dr. Cyberlove:

My online romance suffered a giant setback when she found out that instead of being a 6' 2" intellectual, professional rodeo bronc rider from Maui, I'm actually a 5' 7" balding night clerk from Oshkosh. I'm thinking of giving her a dozen beautiful cyber roses. What do you think?

Signed,
Reality Bytes

Dear Bytes:

Don't be cheap. Give her a cyber Lamborghini or a cyber mansion. If you really want to impress her, give her 85 billion cyber bucks and let her get whatever she wants. Think of how grateful and secure she'll feel. She'll never have to hold down a virtual job again.

• • •

Dear Dr. Cyberlove:

I'm a married man, but I recently met a sexy, fascinating, charming woman in an online chat room. I think I'm in love. What do I tell my wife?

Signed,
Uncertain

Dear Uncertain:

Tell her you've been exchanging sexually explicit messages with a junior high school boy who's pretending to be a thirty-five year old woman. Chances are, that's exactly what's happening.

• • •

Dear Dr. Cyberlove:

When I'm in a chat room with the opposite sex, I can't seem to type a single clever response. Do you have any lines I can use?

Signed,
All Thumbs

Dear Thumbs:

Sure. How about:

Your hard drive or mine?

Hey, I like the size of your vocabulary.

You'll never guess what I'd like to download.

You turn my emoticons upside down.

What's a nice hacker like you doing in a cheap

chat room like this?

♦ ♦ ♦

Dear Dr. Cyberlove:

It seems that many of the people I talk to in the online chat rooms aren't really as they describe themselves. How can I be sure I'm not being misled?

Signed,
Bewitched Bothered and Bewildered

Dear Bewildered:

You can't. Remember that if a man describes himself as "charismatic, adventuresome and a rugged individualist who's not afraid to be different" those words could easily describe Jack the Ripper. Need another example? I'm not really a doctor, I have absolutely no experience in offering romantic advice, and I'm simply doing it as a lark.

♦ ♦ ♦

Dear Dr. Cyberlove:

I'm finished with online romances. I've had three disastrous relationships. Any suggestions about where a person can have better luck in meeting like-minded members of the opposite sex?

Signed,
Looking For Love In All The Wrong Places

Dear Places:

Have you tried bars?

Barbie

I DON'T USUALLY keep up with celebrity birthdays. I have a hard enough time remembering when family members were born.

But I realized that I recently missed the birthday of one of the most beautiful women in the world. I'm referring, of course, to Barbie.

Since her introduction at the 1959 New York Toy Fair, more than 800 million Barbies have been sold. And although her popularity continues to grow, there are some obscure facts that would surprise even the most compulsive Barbie collector.

For example, Barbie began her career as a model, but was so poor at first that she posed for cheesecake photos that can still be seen hanging in the barracks of G.I. Joe.

Over the years, Barbie has held down a number of different jobs. There've been Air Force Pilot Barbie, Baseball Player Barbie, Astronaut Barbie and Rock Star Barbie. But not all attempts have been successful, such as Sister Mary Barbie, Slut Barbie, Obese Barbie, Satan-worshiper Barbie, Acne Barbie and Psycho Killer Barbie.

Through it all, she's maintained her appearance and her figure. And she hardly looks a day older. But it's not been without a cost. Barbie's had seven face-lifts, four nose jobs, three tummy tucks and a couple of cellulite excavations. (For some reason, she was never interested in breast enhancements.)

An eating disorder plagued her off and on through the sixties. During the early seventies, she was stalked by a deranged, one-eyed Mr. Potato Head. A supermarket tabloid claimed that in the mid-eighties she was admitted into the Betty Boop Clinic for substance abuse, but this was never substantiated and is now believed to be just a cheap rumor.

Barbie's real name was Barbara Jo Skank, but she decided to use only a single name on the advice of her agent. Since then, others, like Cher and Madonna, have followed her example.

For a while, a torrid romance between Barbie and Ken had all the makings of a public relations dream—two young, glamorous international stars in love. He promised to build her a dream home out of Lincoln Logs and furnish it with the best that Monopoly money could buy.

But the relationship soon went sour. Her popularity eclipsed his, and he couldn't stand it. One night, in a jealous rage, he trashed 175 of her prom dresses and stomped on her dog Prince.

Ken went directly to jail. (He did not collect $100.) Upon his release, he worked intermittently as a lounge lizard until he was outed in 1997.

There is currently a medical condition known as Barbie Syndrome, which is characterized by a woman's obsession with having huge blond hair and a wasp-like waist. Dollie Parton is a victim of Barbie Syndrome.

Some have accused Barbie of being shallow, even somewhat of a bimbo. And while it's true that there is not a single thought in her head, such charges are mean-spirited and serve no good purpose.

For millions of young girls (and a couple of odd adolescent boys), Barbie has been a role model. She taught them that when they grew up, life could be wonderful and they could be unspeakably happy and successful as long as they were beautiful, always wore a new outfit and were built like a brick outhouse.

Over the decades, Barbie has had her fair share of admirers and critics. Some believe her influence has been healthy. Others question the values she represents. But say what you will, no matter which side you're on, there's one thing you can't deny.

That Barbie—she's a real doll.

The Psychic Fair

WE ARE DRIVING—the lovely Mrs. Borengasser
and I—past a hotel that is hosting a "Psychic Fair."

Unfortunately, I misread the marquee and
think it actually says "Psycho Fair." I quickly floor
the accelerator in an effort to get as far away as
possible from this dangerous place. I realize the
criminally insane deserve their pastimes like
everyone else, but I don't really want to be in the
vicinity.

Moments later, a nice police officer explains
that fleeing psychos is not an acceptable defense
for doing 65 in a 30.

As I tuck my speeding ticket in the glove
compartment, the lovely Mrs. Borengasser
explains that it was actually a "Psychic Fair" and
suggests we check it out.

The Psychic Fair consists of several large rooms
of displays, exhibits, demonstrations and oddly
dressed characters giving "readings." A reading,
as it turns out, is not a recitation of a poem or a
chapter from a new bestseller like you'd get at your
local Barnes & Noble. No, a reading consists of
giving a perfect stranger fifty dollars to guess what

kind of person you are and what will happen to you in two or three months.

There is also a Snack Bar, specializing in healthy eating alternatives, with things like Tofu-on-a-Stick and Ginseng Häagan-Daz.

One booth we visit is nothing but crystals—hundreds and hundreds of crystals. I am pretty well up to my karma in crystals.

When I approach the crystal merchant, he asks, "What's your favorite crystal?"

"Gayle," I reply.

He's puzzled. "What powers does it have?" he finally asks.

"I'm not sure," I say. "But ... but don't it make your brown eyes blue?" It is then that the lovely Mrs. Borengasser inserts her elbow into my ribcage.

At the next booth, a woman steps up and asks, "Are you interested in astral travel?"

"I don't know," I answer. "Is that where you go on a vacation with the entire Houston baseball team?"

"Not the Houston Astros," hisses the lovely Mrs. Borengasser. "Astral. Astral travel is when your mind leaves your body and travels to other places."

I shudder and whisper back, "You mean like what happened to our luggage last trip?"

I turn my attention back to the astral travel

agent. "No, thank you," I tell her. "My mind wanders a little too much as it is."

I stop by a phrenology booth, where a man offers to tell me secrets about myself by feeling the bumps on my head.

"Sure," I agree.

He gropes around on my head for a moment and observes, "This protuberance means you'll have a long fruitful life."

"Ahh ... no disrespect intended, but I think that protuberance means I ought to be more careful getting out of the car."

At one booth, a woman offers to consult my spiritual guide to see what supernatural advice he might have for me.

"No, thanks," I tell her. "After the week I've had, I'm not interested in anything he has to say. Besides, if he was so interested in helping me, he should have let me know that the toilet was going to back up."

As we amble through the Fair, vendors try to sell us healing rocks, books about the paranormal, Tarot cards, biofeedback sessions and conversations with angels, deceased relatives and Nostradamus. It becomes a little overwhelming. And a bit depressing.

Later, on the way home, the lovely Mrs. Borengasser asks, "How'd you like the Psychic Fair?"

"It was okay," I say. "But, now that I've had time to think about it, I might have had more fun at the Psycho Fair."

And if silence is consent, the lovely Mrs. Borengasser agrees.

Theme Restaurants

FIRST, THERE WAS the Hard Rock Café, a theme restaurant with rock and roll paraphernalia all over the place—a gold record here, an old guitar there, a busted drumstick mounted on the wall, and a bronzed groupie by the cash register. This eatery has been so successful that it is now impossible to go more than twenty-four hours without seeing someone wearing a Hard Rock Café shirt.

Unfortunately, what eventually happens is that, as the number of cafés multiplies, the good rock and roll souvenirs become scarcer. I've heard—and this hasn't actually been confirmed—that the newest Hard Rock Café had to make do with a collection of Neil Diamond's collar stays, a stick of spearmint from the 1910 Fruitgum Company and one of the accordions from a performance by Polka Pete and the Bluebonnet Boys.

Nevertheless, this lesson hasn't discouraged other entrepreneurs. Over the years, more theme restaurants have kept appearing, such as Planet Hollywood, the House of Blues, the Fashion Café, Margaritaville, and even an Elvis Presley restaurant.

I haven't actually been to the Elvis Restaurant, but if I were Elvis—and you'll have to take my word that I'm not—I know what I'd want my theme eatery to be like. First, the place would be lousy with Elvi. There'd be Elvis photos on the walls, Elvis records playing nonstop and, everywhere you look, Elvis impersonators. Of course, since this is a restaurant, all the Elvi would have to be Fat Elvi instead of Skinny Elvi. A Skinny Elvis would be bad advertising for a food joint.

In the restaurant, there would be one simple recipe—whatever you order, it'd be dipped in batter and tossed in the deep fry. Everything would be fried—fried meat, fried dough, fried vegetables, fried peanut butter. Even the silverware would have a nice extra-crispy coating.

There would be a Jelly Doughnut *du jour* and a daily Colonel Tom Parker Dessert Special, which would be a gourmet, candy-flavored barbiturate.

Even though many of these ventures have worked out, the theme restaurant concept isn't an automatic blueprint for success. Some have been dismal failures. The Donner Party Diner was an unqualified dud. The Hell Angel's Satan Hole Sushi Bar is not expected to have much of an impact. And the Sermon on the Mount Grill is having a hard time, mostly because of its incredibly limited menu, serving only loaves and fishes.

Suddenly I have a flash of insight. (It could simply be a wave of nausea, but I prefer to give myself the benefit of the doubt.) There's a trend afoot here. Theme restaurants are not limited to grand, wide-sweeping subjects like rock and roll. The theme can be only a person. Like Elvis. After all, many celebrities have started their own restaurants, such as Colonel Sanders and Roy Rogers.

In fact, it may be that during the twenty-first century, at one time or another, everyone will have his or her own restaurant. Even me. That means I have to act fast, before the competition gets too intense. There's not a decade to spare.

At my restaurant, I'll personally meet you at the door. "Welcome to Galaxy Borengasser, a gourmet restaurant dedicated to mayonnaise and everything Borengasser. Your host this evening will be my uncle Raymond, and your waiter will be Doolie, a third cousin on my mother's side. On the way to your table, I'll point out a couple of Borengasser artifacts. Over there is a collection of my gourds. To your immediate left is a bucket of used corks that the lovely Mrs. Borengasser told me I had to get out of the garage.

"Mounted on the wall is a collection of old T-shirts and two pairs of socks. Leaning up against the wine rack is a garden rake. I figured if it was part of the decor, I wouldn't have to use it in the

35

yard this fall."

"Gosh," you'll say, incredibly impressed, "what a terrific place. What's the best thing about having your own theme restaurant? The independence? The money? The fame?"

"Actually, none of those," I'll reply. "The best thing is that I no longer have to throw anything away. I just bring it down here and hang it on the wall."

Growing Old

WHEN ARE YOU an old person? It's becoming more and more difficult to know.

On the one hand, Americans are living longer. Many people in their seventies and eighties are frisky as jackrabbits.

On the other hand, the American Association of Retired Persons, the official organization for coots, accepts membership as early as the age of fifty.

So how can you tell when you're old? Here are some reliable signs:

If you refer to Methuselah as "that young pup."

If your next birthday party will be hosted by the nice folks at Ripley's Believe It or Not.

If you're not allowed to an R-rated movie without a paramedic.

If you're the poster person for the National Prune Council.

If you're dating an eighty-year-old and people accuse you of "robbing the cradle."

If you went to your high school reunion and you were the only one there.

If your birthday cake looked as if it had been hit with napalm.

If you consider driving at fifteen miles per hour "thrill-seeking."

If your favorite Thanksgiving was "that one with the Indians at Plymouth."

If you have to look up the meaning of the word "teeth."

If you're a woman and you think the Chippendales are a couple of Disney rodents.

If you're a man and you need a doctor's permission to watch HBO.

If you get tired from blinking.

If you think Victoria's Secret is something the Queen whispered to an attendant.

If your hearing isn't what it used to be—five minutes ago.

If you think popular music started going downhill with "that young punk, Guy Lombardo."

If, last year, "auld acquaintance were forgot."

If your idea of aerobics is rocking.

If you have great, great, great, great, great grandchildren.

If bouillon seems chewy.

If you're no longer "a geezer."

If naps wear you out.

If your name and the word "relic" are frequently used together.

If you think Rush Limbaugh is too liberal.

If you can't remember the last time you remembered.

If you have to use an orthopedic handkerchief.

If glaciers seem too impetuous and madcap.

If your car has a bumper sticker that says, "Ask Me About My Rheumatism."

If your favorite song is one you heard in an elevator.

If white bread is too spicy.

If you have trouble keeping up with ninety-year-olds.

If you smile and people tell you that you have "a nice set of gums."

If you get junk mail addressed to "Old Fuddy Duddy."

If you're no longer a senior citizen, but have actually begun receiving an "ancient citizen" discount.

Don't worry if several of these conditions apply to you. You still may not have to be classified as an old person. After all, you're only as young as you feel. (Unfortunately, if you feel 130, you're out of luck.)

And how do you maintain your youth? Well, you can consider cryogenics or a stair master or beta-carotene or a tummy tuck or yoga. There are hundreds of salves and schemes and pills, all promising to invigorate you and prolong your life.

But for my money, nothing makes you feel as youthful as standing next to someone who's even older.

Diary of a Vegetarian

Sunday:

I decide to become a vegetarian. And why not? After all, it seems to be the required diet of a guru, a guy who doesn't have to do anything more than perch on the top of a mountain and explain the meaning of life. He doesn't have to shave, and he has disciples. I've always wanted disciples.

Monday:

Nothing to it. A salad for lunch. Spaghetti and a salad for dinner. No visions or inner peace yet, but it's just the first day. You can't rush spiritual enlightenment.

Tuesday:

Another salad for lunch. I think something's starting to happen. I break out in a cold sweat when I accidentally touch a package of bacon bits. Supper consists of a salad and a potato. Later that evening I watch a ballgame and don't really care who wins. Something's definitely starting to happen.

Wednesday:
Another salad for lunch. But I have my first hallucination ... ah ... I mean, vision. All the ballpoints in the office begin to look like Slim Jims. For dinner, I have a salad and a plate of nachos. At 2:00 AM, I sneak into the bathroom and gargle a glass of bouillon. I don't swallow any, though.

Thursday:
Another salad for lunch. Impulsively, on the way home I buy a pet chicken and name him "Drumstick." For supper I have a salad and a veggie casserole. That evening I begin wearing a beach towel on my head and referring to myself as Mahatma Borengasser.

Friday:
Another salad for lunch. I notice that meat eaters look at me differently. Neighborhood dogs either avoid me altogether or sneer at me in disgust. I am no longer fit company for predators. Supper is a salad and six ears of corn. I have my first fainting spell. Mystic revelation can't be far off.

Saturday:
I slip into an altered state of consciousness. When I come to, I'm in a local restaurant, eating prime rib with a side order of fried chicken and

medium rare bacon. I suddenly realize that eating meat for the first time in five days is the closest to a mystic experience that I'm going to get. And that's okay with me.

Liberals

HELLO, BOYS AND GIRLS.

I'm afraid I have some bad news.

There's a serious threat to the future of the United States, and it could be coming from your very own parents. They could be liberals.

Liberalism is like acne. Many people experience it when they're young, but it eventually clears up and goes away. However, there are many liberal rogues still out there, and your parents could be among them.

Here are several ways to tell if your parents are liberal:

Are they idealistic and enthusiastic for change? This is a sure sign of liberalism.

Does your dad wear wild ties?

Do they discuss "ideas"?

Do they still play their old hard rock albums? (They should be concentrating on Big Band Era recordings and easy listening radio stations.)

Do they mention "the status quo" and "intellectual stagnation" as if these are bad things?

Are the names of Republican members of the House and Senate always preceded by words your parents forbid you to use in front of Grandpa and Grandma?

Even though your parents should be conservatives by now, it's difficult to go cold turkey on liberalism and become right-wingers over night, boys and girls. They'll have to enter a halfway program where they become moderates for a year or two.

This won't be easy. Many well-known Democratic politicians have attempted to be moderates with only mixed success.

One of the problems is that everyone hates moderates because they're always so inconsistent and sensible. Being sensible is why it's so hard for a politician to be a moderate. In fact, other expressions for "sensible politician" are "one-termer" and "lame duck."

Moderates also say ridiculous things like "I understand your viewpoint" and "I can appreciate both sides of the issue." Although this may sound good at first, it doesn't make them any friends in the long run.

During this de-tox period, be patient. Even though the moderate road is rough and rocky, the day will come when your parents will become full-fledged, card-carrying conservatives. And won't that be a happy day, boys and girls?

What can you do? How can you help?

It's easy. If you suspect that your parents are liberals, call one of the many conservative watchdog organizations and report your findings. You'll be helping this great country of ours rid itself of these pesky liberals. Plus you'll immediately receive ten free videos, ten free music downloads and have a chance to win dozens of other terrific prizes, including a trip to Disney World.

And don't worry, kids. No one will hurt your folks. They won't be flogged or put in leg chains. This is, after all, twenty-first century America. The sixties are long past.

Your parents will be treated humanely. They are only being identified as liberals for future indoctrination and deprogramming. (If they resist, they may be brought down with a stun gun, but that's the worst.)

It might make you feel better to know that this initial phase is patterned after our country's highly successful wildlife management program.

In other words, boys and girls, once your parents are subdued, they'll simply be tagged and released.

Mother Nature

IT'S NIGHT.

The lovely Mrs. Borengasser and I are driving home.

As we approach our driveway, she spots a shape moving across our front yard. "I think that's a skunk," she says.

I pull sideways across the road and point my headlights at the critter.

Sure enough, a skunk.

I get out of the car and circle the skunk to try and encourage him to leave the premises. We have a No Loitering Policy for animals in our yard, which is strictly enforced. In fact, it's modeled after the one at the Mall of America in Minneapolis.

Skunks don't run. They waddle. And this one waddles over near the front door of our house and then—I can't believe it—slips down into a hole under our sidewalk. The reality hits me like a noxious odor. We have a skunk living right outside our front door.

Mother Nature is usually depicted as a loving, generous, matronly female. Nothing could be further from the truth. This is merely a Madison

Avenue trick, like taking a ferocious flesh-eating tiger, naming him Tony and then using him to sell cereal. In truth, Mother Nature is a shameless, gap-toothed old crone who delights in creating havoc.

What do you expect from someone who hangs around with that sodden backwoods bum, Old Man River? Ask anyone. They'll tell you that he don't know nothing. He just keeps rolling along. There have been rumors about the two of them for years.

The skunk is only the latest of Old Lady Nature's minions to invade our area. We've had birds build nests in the dryer air duct and block it up with twigs. Woodpeckers have pecked holes in our house along the roof line and squirrels (a.k.a. tree weasels) then used these as entrances into our attic. Once a swarm of bees relocated into the space between our interior and exterior walls. Another time, a possum began dining on our cat's food and finally moved into our cat shelter. During storms, trees hurl limbs at the house.

Do you know what a pileated woodpecker is? A field guide will tell you that it's a striking bird, about seventeen inches long, a bit of a recluse and that, if you see one at close range, "consider yourself privileged." What the field guide won't tell you is that the pileated woodpecker was the model for Woody Woodpecker, an insane bird that is little more than a flying jackhammer.

A week ago, I heard a loud noise outside the house. I went to the living room and there, on the post between two windows, was a pileated woodpecker ripping up our window casing. Just for the sheer joy of destruction. Oh, the pileated woodpecker is a striking bird all right. It'll strike your house, your garage and your tool shed.

And, now we have a resident skunk, an animal that has the choice of either spraying you with the most noxious fumes in nature or giving you rabies.

How do you get rid of a skunk? Rap music? Opera? Bagpipes? A bottle of cologne? Dynamite? What if it's a mother skunk and there are baby skunks down there? I live in a country that celebrates Mother's Day, so I can hardly endanger their foul-smelling little lives.

You're probably saying, "What do you expect, living in the country?" Well, we don't live in the country. We live in town, surrounded by neighbors. I'm quite certain that if we actually lived in the country, bears would be picking their teeth with my femur and using my head for an impromptu soccer game.

So, don't sing me the praises of Mother Nature. As far as I'm concerned, she's a witch on wheels. I'm sure that at this very instant, she's plotting the next assault on our home. I'm not sure what it'll be—we may be infested by fleas or besieged by grackles or flattened by a tree. And I don't know when—it could be five minutes from now or next year.

All I do know is that when the dust settles, I'll hear the old hag cackling.

The Cabbage Soup Diet

THE LOVELY Mrs. Borengasser reads about a miracle diet, called the Cabbage Soup Diet, which claims you can lose ten to seventeen pounds in seven days.

We decide to give it a try. The diet only lasts a week. How bad can it be?

Day One Menu: Only fruit and as much cabbage soup as you want. No bananas.

I begin the day with a celebratory apple. Quite satisfying. Late morning, I have my first bowl of cabbage soup. Not bad, especially with the help of a little pepper sauce. This diet's going to be a piece of cake (an unfortunate choice of words that gives me my first twinge of regret). But it's a momentary lapse. I have a second helping of soup and regain my enthusiasm. I remind myself that one week from today, people will be describing me as "svelte" and "petite."

Day Two Menu: Only fresh vegetables and as much cabbage soup as you want. No peas, beans or corn, but we can each have one buttered baked potato.

I quickly discover why raw broccoli isn't a standard breakfast item. By noon, I've eaten so many carrots that I catch myself answering the phone with, "Ehhh, what's up, Doc?" I have a couple bowls of cabbage soup for lunch. The rest of the day I spend fantasizing about the baked potato with butter that I'll have for dinner, mostly about the butter. That evening, the lovely Mrs. Borengasser and I glare at each other's potato with unabashed envy.

Day Three Menu: Fruits and vegetables and as much cabbage soup as you want. No bananas or potatoes.

I've come to hate the words, "as much cabbage soup as you want," which is beginning to mean "none." At the park, a miniature Chihuahua, hardly the size of a sewer rat, sneers at me. I'm obviously losing my place in the food chain. I also notice that the diet affects my mood. I feel like Snow White's eighth dwarf, Psycho. And the lovely Mrs. Borengasser isn't exactly in the running for Miss Congeniality.

Day Four Menu: It's banana day. Eight bananas, unlimited skim milk and, of course, the vile cabbage soup.

I've never had eight bananas in a single day. It's an unnatural quantity. I know orangutans who don't eat eight bananas in a day. In desperation, I put my last three bananas in a blender with skim milk in a feeble attempt to make a smoothie. It's like eating a runny banana. But at least it isn't cabbage soup.

The lovely Mrs. Borengasser and I are becoming increasingly irritable and snappish. When she refers to me as "lamb chop" and "cupcake," I take it as a thinly veiled effort to torment me with the names of yummy foods. In retaliation, I call her "my little bacon double cheeseburger with extra mayo," and we don't speak to each other for the rest of the night. I blame it on the bananas.

Day Five Menu: Beef, chicken or fish, six tomatoes and the cabbage gruel.

I've been waiting on this moment since Day One. At last. Real protein. I eat a can of tuna fish and a tomato at 5:30 in the morning and pass out from pure pleasure.

That evening, I bring home fried chicken instead of roasted, thinking we can simply peel off the fried batter. But on this diet, anything fried is the Chow of Satan, crust or no crust. The lovely Mrs. Borengasser feels that I've committed some terrible, unforgivable atrocity. It's the first time I've ever seen her snarl.

Day Six Menu: Beef, chicken or fish, leafy greens and cabbage swill.

And *Day Seven Menu:* Brown rice, vegetables, unsweetened fruit juice and—shudder—cabbage soup.

These last two days are a blur, as I drift in and out of consciousness. But the week is finally over.

Looking back, I realize the Cabbage Soup Diet, though difficult, wasn't totally without merit.

We each lost eight pounds.

Also, in this age of mile-a-minute hustle and bustle, we found a way to bring time to a screeching halt. Because when you're on the Cabbage Soup Diet, a week lasts forever.

And when one of life's setbacks threatens to ruin our day, all we have to say is, "Hey, at least it ain't cabbage soup."

Most of all, the lovely Mrs. Borengasser and I discovered that the Cabbage Soup Diet truly is a miracle diet. The miracle is that we didn't kill each other.

Molly's Pups

OKAY. LET'S SAY you're a conscientious parent. You and your spouse are doing your best to raise your children to become good, wholesome, responsible adults. One kid is giving you joy and fulfillment. The other is giving you ulcers. She's got more tattoos than a Hell's Angel, pierced body parts you don't want to think about and spiked hair of a color not found in nature.

Or perhaps you're an honest, hard-working single parent. You're sitting at home, watching TV and admiring the delightful artwork your daughter made especially for you. Something catches your eye on the television screen. You notice that the sniper on the 6:00 PM news looks familiar. He should. He's your oldest son.

How is this possible? Too much discipline? Bad companions? Not enough roughage?

Where did you go wrong? What could you have done differently? Are you absolutely worthless as a parent? As a person? As a life form? Before you beat yourself up any more about this, let me tell you about Molly's pups.

Molly was a mixed breed dog, part terrier, part God-knows-what, that we bought on impulse from a pet shop. Mostly white, with a few dark splotches, she was already six months old when we got her. She was a bundle of energy, extremely nervous and high-strung. To make sure we understood this, she threw up twice before we even made it out of the parking lot.

But over the next few months, her digestive system settled down. She turned out to be smart and affectionate and, before long, we were all getting along just fine.

One evening, a fence-jumping, mixed-breed, rogue male dog leaped into her pen and took the necessary steps to start her on the road to motherhood. A few months later, Molly had a family.

What we didn't realize at the time was that Molly was not only a full-time canine mother and homemaker. She was also a career woman. She was contributing invaluable work as a biologist, specifically a geneticist.

She accomplished this, not by publishing an academic paper or experimenting with garden peas, but by bearing eight pups—Buster, Snow White, Mort, Waggedy Ann, Brownie, Butch, Calvin and Venus.

From the moment of birth, each one of Molly's pups was dramatically different. Butch, solid brown, was a bully. Calvin, black and white, was rebellious and continually fought with his mother.

Mort, white with brown and black spots, got along with everybody. Brownie, brown and incredibly fuzzy, slept nonstop. Snow White, solid white, was hyperactive and independent. Venus was the cutest, just a slip of a thing. Buster was big and lumbering, a good ol' boy in a puppy suit. And, of course, Waggedy Ann wagged.

It had nothing to do with whether the pups watched too much television (they didn't), whether their father deserted them (he did), whether Molly was too permissive (she may have been) or whether a conservative presidential candidate criticized her on national television for being a single parent (he/she didn't). The DNA simply got tossed into the genetic blender, it was switched to frappé, and we ended up with a Whitman's Sampler of personalities, eight totally unique pups.

Molly was a great mother—patient, understanding, loving. She treated all her children the same. If you asked her which pup was her favorite, she would have told you (if she could talk, of course) that she loved them all equally. The fact that one of them will eventually chew the leg off a postman, another will save a drowning child and still another will kill cats for recreation is completely out of her paws. If a pup develops multiple personalities or becomes a mad dog killer, it's not Molly's fault. They were born different. They'll remain different.

There is an ongoing scientific debate about the impact of heredity versus environment, nature versus nurture. Well, you can forget Gregor Mendel, George Washington Carver and anybody else who has some half-baked genetic theory. They were right, of course, but it was Molly and her pups who proved conclusively, once and for all, that it is heredity and nature that determine a youngster's temperament and, ultimately, his or her future.

So, if you have a difficult child, don't despair. You may not be to blame.

Like Molly's pups, your child's character and disposition could be simply an accident of birth. A genetic crap shoot.

Your kid's problems may have little to do with his or her environment.

On the other hand, you may just be a really lousy parent.

Smoking

IT'S THE YEAR 2020.

As everyone knows, for the last few years, America has been embroiled in a controversy that has completely split the nation. As a result, the country was officially divided into smoking and non-smoking zones.

The western United States was declared a non-smoking area. All the states east of the Mississippi River are smoking states. A slim strip of states in the Midwest have been maintained as secondhand smoking regions, inhabited mostly by people who are trying to quit. The one exception is Texas, which was declared a Chawin' State.

Even the most enthusiastic supporters of this system admit it can be slightly inconvenient. For instance, if you work in Utah and are dying for a smoke, you have to drive to Kentucky to light up.

Or if you're driving the kids to Disney World and you keep seeing billboards advising you that Florida may be hazardous to your health, it's going to put a crimp in your vacation.

A Bob Dylan concert had to be moved from California to New York because there weren't enough Bic lighters for the customary salute.

When foreigners enter the country, immigration officials have to say, "Welcome to America. What is your destination—smoking or non-smoking?"

Historians trace the origin of the anti-tobacco movement back to the early 1990s, when politicians were frantically searching for some politically safe cause to champion. Drugs seemed a natural at first, but it was too difficult. A "Just Say No" campaign was so ineffective that it was eventually changed to "Just Say Not Now."

Alcohol also seemed a likely candidate, but prohibition hadn't worked. So the government finally settled on tobacco.

Over the years, the smoking and anti-smoking factions became so bitter towards each other that the only way to avoid outright violence was to split the country into smoking and non-smoking sections. This extreme measure seemed to be working until last week, when the Illinois National Guard, led by General Joseph Camel, moved into Iowa and declared it a smoking area. In a scene reminiscent of Iwo Jima, the R. J. Reynolds flag was erected in downtown Dubuque. Wyoming retaliated by capturing Nebraska, converting it to a non-smoking zone and hanging the Marlboro Man in effigy in an Omaha Exxon station.

The Surgeon General, Commander of the Non-smoking Forces, is reportedly furious, vowing to end the insurrection at any cost. He's training an army of special troops, guerrilla fighters who'll be armed with water pistols, with orders to "shoot to extinguish." A team of secret agents are planning to infiltrate the smoking states, leaving 8" by 10" glossies of smokers' lungs behind the windshield wipers of mall shoppers. There's even a terrible rumor that he plans to drop the big one on North Carolina—an enormous nicotine patch. He refers to it as "a nicotine patch for the nicotine patch."

The smokers will surely retaliate. In fact, for the last two days, giant smoke rings have been seen drifting over the Rockies. Also, a large puffy cloud is moving across the Midwest towards Colorado. And, even worse, it smells like menthol. If the sunlight is blocked for an extended period of time, life on the West Coast will be threatened.

An armed clash between the two factions is considered inevitable in what is being called the Second War Between the States. No doubt there will be many skirmishes with tragic repercussions. For instance, it's said that anyone caught smoking within ten blocks of a federal building will be considered a war criminal. Repeat offenders could be shot by a firing squad. The upside is that firing squad etiquette requires that they be offered a last cigarette.

Will we be able to stop this divisive conflict in time? Will the two sides be able to compromise and coexist once again?

Maybe so, but not by smoking a peace pipe.

Holiday Food

CHRISTMAS IS supposedly the most stressful holiday. Thanksgiving is second. Between these two holidays are four weeks of overeating, when the average person will gain ten pounds.

How can you avoid it? You can't. There will be Thanksgiving leftovers. Coworkers will bring food to work. Friends and relatives will give you food as gifts. And, of course, you'll be preparing more food at home.

So, as long as you're going to overeat anyway, you might as well do it as quickly and efficiently as possible. As a public service, I'm offering these fool-proof holiday recipes and cooking tips.

It wouldn't be proper to begin any discussion of holiday food without honoring the venerable green bean casserole. As anyone older than three and a half knows, combining green beans, cream of mushroom soup and onion rings is the basic recipe for the classic green bean casserole, which has become so universal that no one in the United States will be able to make it from Thanksgiving to Christmas without being served it at least once. If you host a potluck dinner, at least 35% of the people will show up with green bean casseroles.

Holiday depression can often be traced directly back to an absence of green bean casserole. In fact, the ultimate holiday experience is to eat an entire green bean casserole while watching *It's a Wonderful Life*.

This formula is such a winner it can be applied to other items as well. Take anything you find in the refrigerator, in the cupboard or even on the floor, mix it with a can of cream of mushroom soup and top with a couple handfuls of onion rings. Bake at 350 degrees for forty minutes. Voila! A killer casserole (figuratively speaking). (Note: For variety, try cream of chicken, cream of celery or any of the other "cream of" soups. It won't taste any different, but at least you'll feel as if you're varying the menu.)

Dips are popular holiday fare for get-togethers with family and friends. A simple method is to mix a container of sour cream with any dried soup mix. Dip anything in it—crackers, veggies, a spare tire, pruning shears, even (shudder) low fat potato chips.

Frying is a great way to use up leftovers. Take any item, from an entire cow to an old boot, plunge in batter and fry it. (Note: The actual item you cook is unimportant since frying is only an excuse to eat the fried batter. In fact, this is actually a good way to recycle cardboard.)

A delicious party treat is Batter-on-a-Stick.

Simply dip a popsicle stick in batter and fry, dip and fry, etc., until you get the size you like. (Once you become proficient at this process, you can also make candles.)

Here are some additional cooking tips to make your efforts in the kitchen tastier and much easier:

Take any combination of leftovers from the fridge and mix them together. Serve them cold and call it a salad. Serve them hot with rice and call it stir fry. Serve them in beef broth and call it stew.

Remember: you'll always be okay as long as you never run out of mayonnaise or peanut butter.

When in doubt, apply more salt.

There are two miracle ingredients (in addition to the previously mentioned mayonnaise and peanut butter) that can save any culinary disaster—a melted stick of butter and bacon. And, of course, a green bean casserole.

I suppose it's not surprising that we're so preoccupied with food over these two stressful holidays. After all, what does the average American do when stressed out? Overeat. And what happens when you overeat? You gain weight and get more stressed out.

It's a delicious circle.

Rules of Travel

THE LOVELY Mrs. Borengasser and I recently left the country. Happily, it wasn't at the request of the State Department. We were going on a vacation to a small island in the Caribbean. As a result of that trip, we've developed a list of rules for traveling abroad.

Never believe a travel brochure.
According to travel brochures, the sun always shines, and the natives all think you're the greatest thing since sliced guava. Your destination is a place where dreams come true. Dreams come true all right, especially if you're dreaming of gale force winds, surly service and prices higher than Mount McKinley. In brochure-speak, "overlooking the ocean" means you're on the side of a mountain and you can see the water with a pair of military binoculars. "Romantic hideaway" means inaccessible by normal modes of transportation. "Rustic charm" means no electricity.

Never fly in a plane so small you can't stand up.
Our airplane was tiny and battered. Picture a go-cart with wings. It had been through some hard

times, like maybe World War I. There were only seven passenger seats. I knew we were in trouble when the pilot asked who wanted to ride shotgun. I didn't feel any better when I noticed the fuzzy dice hanging over the instrument panel. All the passengers looked nervous. I tried to lighten the mood by asking if this was a dinner flight. To teach me a lesson, Captain Tailspin took away my life vest, parachute and flare gun.

Never be rude to a customs official.
Customs is like the IRS in a nasty mood. This is what can occur: a customs officer wakes up with a crick in his neck. Later, you happen to come through his inspection station. Still feeling generally irritable, he orders you to sing "Climb Every Mountain" while being strip-searched. He can do this because a customs official has absolute power. If he wishes, he can make you and your fellow passengers Hokey Pokey across the tarmac. Be nice to this man. He can have you imprisoned for scowling or shot for sneezing.

Don't plan anything on your day of arrival.
This is because there's a good chance it won't really be your day of arrival, especially if you're flying on a small airline. Small airlines figure that if you were that serious about getting to your destination on time, you would have flown

on a real airplane. On our trip, we were bumped
from one flight and taken to another agent to be
rerouted. He quickly stamped our tickets and said
urgently, "Go now! Now! Go right now!"

"When does our flight leave?" I asked.

"Now! Right now!"

This is a trick. Nothing happens "now" in an
airport. Everything has either already occurred or
will transpire in twenty minutes. Airline personnel
always use increments of twenty minutes because
research has shown that twenty minutes is the
maximum delay that the average person will
accept without going ballistic.

**Never lose your luggage in a foreign country.
Never. Never. Never.**
An airline once lost my luggage for four days. By
the third day, strangers were offering me rides
to the laundromat and giving me gift certificates
for Arrid Extra Dry. Street people avoided making
eye contact with me. On this trip, our luggage
was missing for two days. We finally located our
suitcases sitting in a completely different airport
more than fifty miles away—stuck in customs.
When I asked the customs official if there had
been a problem, he simply shrugged and told me
they hadn't liked the color of my shirt.

PCP Anonymous

THE HOTEL SUITE is full, with twenty or so people sitting in a circle.

I know none of them.

I take a seat.

In the center of the circle is a moderator.

One at a time, each person stands up, facing everyone else, and makes his or her announcement.

Soon it's my turn.

I rise and solemnly say, "My name is Dan Borengasser, and I'm a recovering Politically Correct Person."

What led to such a predicament?

Thanks for asking.

It all happened just last month—

The lovely Mrs. Borengasser and I are talking, and, without thinking, I refer to our daughter, little Alice, as a woman. *A woman.*

I am appalled. I've been so conditioned by the politically correct movement that I automatically call our nine-year-old child a woman. I realize that I now live in a world where girls are women, waiters are waitpersons and midgets are height-challenged.

Everyone has become too thin-skinned and hypersensitive, like hothouse flowers that shrink from contact.

I have to be deprogrammed. A friend tells me about PCPA—Politically Correct Persons Anonymous—and I attend my first meeting.

The moderator is calling on me. He shows me a picture.

"This person weighs 300 pounds," he says. "How would you describe him?"

"Cellulite-gifted?" I venture.

He shakes his head. "Try again."

"Big-boned?"

"You know better than that," he chides.

"Hefty? Ponderous? Leviathan?"

"Come on," he encourages. "You're almost there. You can do it."

I break out in a cold sweat. My breath comes in gasps. As my eyes dart uncomfortably about, I notice that my group is eagerly watching me, encouraging me. Finally, I hit the wall: "Fat," I yell. "He's fat. That man is fat as a hog."

Suddenly, I feel an incredible wave of relief, as if some terrible burden had been lifted from me.

He nods enthusiastically. "Good. Good. You've

just taken the first step to recovery."

Over the next several weeks, I eat veal, buy something that's not made in America, chop down a tree, smoke a cigar in public, try on a fur coat, make leather thongs and tell jokes about women and minorities. Everyone gets an opportunity to make fun of my heritage and my religion.

Does it work? Am I deprogrammed?

I don't know.

Then one day I catch myself snickering at a woman buying tofu. I begin to fondly recall old stereotypes. Perhaps there's hope.

But later that afternoon, I scowl at a man who looks up at a tall woman and says, "How's the weather up there, Beanpole?"

I become incredibly depressed. Maybe my PCPA training just didn't take. I'll be doomed to a life of vapid thoughtfulness.

But that night at a party, I tell a Polish joke.

I think I may make it.

Road Rage

ROAD RAGE can be a frightening phenomenon, causing drivers to get so furious that they'll become overly aggressive and, in some cases, violent.

I know about road rage. I've had a case of it myself from time to time. So I'm well qualified to answer some frequently asked questions about it.

Question: I was recently riding my bicycle along the road, was knocked down by a passing car and slid across the pavement, which really made me angry. Is this road rage?

Answer: No, this is actually road rash (which probably doesn't make it any less annoying).

Question: An incredibly rude driver cut me off during rush hour traffic. Do I qualify for road rage?

Answer: Sorry, no. Road rage is not something you just jump into. You have to work your way up to it, like becoming an Eagle Scout. First, you must go through road irk, then road peeve, followed by road testy, road rancor and road wrath, till you're finally eligible for road rage. If you don't take the necessary steps, you'll find yourself doing aggressively inappropriate things, like screaming at the odometer, making spit bubbles or performing some bizarre Three Stooges hand gesture.

Question: Is road rage contagious?

Answer: Good question. Yes, road rage is contagious. It can be transmitted by obscene gestures, loud cursing, horn honking and sideswiping.

Question: How can I tell if I have road rage?

Answer: You most likely are experiencing road rage if you look in the rear view mirror and your face is beet red and you realize you've stopped breathing. Or if you suddenly find yourself groping for your assault rifle. Or if you glance at the passenger seat, see yourself sitting there and realize that you're beside yourself.

Question: Are there other types of common rage besides road rage?

Answer: Yes, indeed. There's parking lot rage, when someone suddenly pulls into your parking space. There's revenue office rage, when you realize that renewing your car tags will take the better part of a week. And, of course, there's supermarket rage, when the person in front of you in the less-than-ten-items-check-out has a whole cart full of groceries and wants to cash a third-party check.

Question: Is this kind of behavior a new phenomenon?

Answer: Not really. When Robin Hood and Little John tried to cross a stream at the same time, it quickly escalated into bridge rage and then erupted into violence. And if you ever saw the movie *Ben Hur*, you'll remember that much of the movie was about coliseum rage, focusing on a dozen really rude chariot drivers.

Question: Is becoming extremely angry unhealthy?

Answer: Not necessarily. Rage can clean out your system. Like a car that's only driven in the city, your body can build up dangerous hydrocarbons and become sluggish. Rage blows out the soot, as it were.

Question: I've read that if you honk your horn more than twice a week, you have a problem. Is this true?

Answer: Absolutely. It means you're living in an area populated by crummy drivers. But at least you know your horn is working.

Question: How can I keep from being a victim of road rage?

Answer: There are many methods. For example, you can wear blinders or take a bus. Some people have tried meditation, but it is extremely important to meditate with your eyes open. One surefire way is if you're ever in front of me, don't drive like an idiot.

Leftovers

THE TERM "leftover" comes from an ancient Greek word meaning, "maybe it'll taste better tomorrow."

That's fine, but most of the time at our house, leftovers are not just left over. They're left over and over and over and over and over. Here's how it works—

We go out for a pizza and bring back a third of it to snack on later. Then we forget about it. Six weeks later, we find it in the very back of the refrigerator, looking like nuclear waste, with a half-life of 1,500 years.

The lovely Mrs. Borengasser is sensitive about the subject. "Did you know," I ask her, " that there's something in the lettuce crisper that is black, has fur and throbs?"

"Oh, yeah," she says. "I think that's either half an avocado or a chicken wing."

"Don't we have to have some sort of license to create new life forms," I ask tactfully.

"Don't be silly," she replies. "We can give it to the dog."

"More likely, we'd be giving the dog to it."

The lovely Mrs. Borengasser ignores me.

"Oh, sure," I continue, "it's easy to slough it off now, but just wait. Some day, when we least expect it, a mutant tuna casserole that's a little smarter, a little more advanced, will rise up out of its Tupperware and come looking for us. Then, it won't be so funny."

I let this sink in before going on. "And, there's a blueberry muffin in there that looks as if it's been carpeted."

"Hey, bacteria have to eat, too."

"Fine," I agree. "Then let them chip in on the groceries."

Perhaps when you think of spoiled food, you think of green cheese or Technicolor meat. Ha! Green cheese is a delicacy. Technicolor meat? Zesty.

Our leftovers are in another league. That's because we don't actually eat leftovers. We raise them.

I still remember the first time I dug out some old lettuce and found that it had liquefied. I had truly lost my innocence.

That's usually what happens to leftovers, a nightmarish alchemy where solids turn into liquids, and liquids turn into solids.

Maybe we wouldn't have such a problem if we made a real effort to eat leftovers sooner. And I'm willing to help. I'll do my share. In fact, I'll go to the fridge right now for a snack.

Hmmm ... what'll it be?

I know. I'll have a glass of lettuce and a slice of milk.

License Tags

IT'S 4:00 AM Tuesday morning. I'm in the kitchen.
The lovely Mrs. Borengasser, hearing me rooting
around, has awakened and come downstairs.

"What on earth are you doing down here at this
hour?" she asks. "Are you feeling all right?"

"I'm getting ready," I respond.

"Ready for what?"

"This is the day I'm renewing my driver's license."

"I still don't understand," she says.

I show her a thick legal pad of calculations.
"After years of observation, I think I finally have
it figured out," I tell her. "My theory is that I will
have to wait in line the minimum amount of time
if I show up at exactly 9:45 AM on the Tuesday
before the last day of the month."

"You figured that out, did you?" she asks,
sounding somewhat skeptical.

"Yes, indeed. And, for your information, during
a presidential election year, the optimum time
seems to be 10:15 AM instead of 9:45. Don't ask me
why.

"I've thought it all out this year," I assure
her. "This backpack has my rations, trail mix and
PowerAde, to make sure I get enough nutrients

to keep up my strength. This duct tape around my wrist is to remind me not to lock my knees. I've heard that if you pass out in line, they'll just drag you out back and you'll lose your place. I've also got a newspaper, a couple of magazines and several novels to help me while away the hours."

"What's in the satchel?" she asks.

"Those are my official papers. You know how there's always three or four things you absolutely have to have to get a renewal? Receipts and forms and affidavits and such? Well, this year, I'm prepared. I've got everything here—check stubs from the last seven years, citizenship papers, fishing license, high school diploma. Whatever they want, I've got it. This year, I'm ready!"

9:45 AM: I arrive at the license renewal office. My calculations were accurate. There are only thirty-five people ahead of me. I begin reading *War and Peace*.

11:00 AM: Two people have fainted in the last fifteen minutes. I feel bad for them, but I do get to move up in line. I'm twentieth now.

12:00 noon: Things have slowed down. The one employee on duty has taken a break. I eat a little dried fruit and do some deep breathing exercises. I'm nineteenth.

2:00 PM: A couple of us join forces to unnerve the people ahead of us. We say things like, "I hear they're closing today at 2:30" and "You know you have to pay with cash and have exact change, don't you?" and "You don't have to worry if you don't get your tags today; the police have a 30-day grace period for expired licenses." It works. Three people leave. I'm tenth in line.

3:30 PM: I'm running out of time. The employee is on break again, and there are still six people ahead of me.

4:25 PM: I'm in trouble. They close in five minutes, and there's a woman with a small child in front of me. Desperate times demand desperate measures. I ask the woman if she has any aspirin because my hepatitis is acting up. She dashes out. I get my tags renewed.

That evening, the lovely Mrs. Borengasser meets me at the door. "How'd it go?"

"Not bad," I say, proudly holding up my renewed license. "And, this year, I didn't even need a paramedic."

Pet Psychiatrist

I RECENTLY read an article about a pet psychiatrist, a doctor who treats the neuroses and psychoses of household pets.

I thought about this for a nanosecond. I've got plenty of problems of my own and I'm going to pay for my dog to go to a shrink? Sorry, Fido. Not in this lifetime.

Besides, what kind of anxieties can a pet have? Our dog sometimes has episodes of binge eating, and then she throws up. But usually it's from eating a pound or two of grass or a dead toad. So bulimic she's not. Her biggest daily trauma is figuring out how to get more table scraps. Not exactly the stuff of *One Flew Over the Cuckoo's Nest*.

But considering it for another nanosecond, I realize that there's money to be made here. After all, how hard can this be? I didn't need any certification. There's no university or medical school offering a degree in pet psychiatry. Not even in California. So, if I say I'm a pet psychiatrist, who's to say differently? You? Hah!

And if I make the wrong diagnosis, who's going to complain? Little Fluffy? Hardly.

My next move is obvious. I rent office space, put

out a sign and wait for the customers to pour in.

My first patient is a dachshund. His owner tells me, "My dog's name is Max and he's subject to dramatic mood swings. I think he may have an inferiority complex."

"Of course, he has an inferiority complex," I sneer in disbelief. "He's a weenie dog. He is inferior. There's only one thing you can do."

"What's that, Doc?"

"Get rid of him. Thank you. Pay the receptionist on the way out."

I prop my feet up on my desk. Wow, I think, this job is going to be a snap.

My next patient is a black Labrador named Hank.

"What seems to be the problem," I ask, "other than the fact that a Lab is as dumb as a post?"

The woman who brought him in explains, "Hank frequently bites my husband. Any ideas, Doctor?"

"You bet. Hank has a serious Oedipus complex. For the next few months, your husband will have to walk around the house in drag. I suggest a blond wig, a little mascara, and a matching skirt and blouse. Hank will eventually become accustomed to your husband and no longer view him as a competitor for your affection. Unfortunately, neither will you."

"Gosh, that seems severe. Are there any other solutions?"

"Yeah. Get rid of him."

"Which one? Hank or my husband?"

"Your choice."

Next is a Siamese cat named Jasmine. Her owner tells me, "Jasmine is sometimes sweet, sometimes bashful, and at other times, nasty tempered. I'm afraid she may have multiple personalities. You know, like Sybil."

"Lady," I explain with much impatience, "let's not forget that this is a cat we're talking about. There's barely room in there for one personality. Much less two."

"But what can I do?"

"Get rid of her. Find a less complicated pet with a more pleasant disposition."

"Like what?"

"A gerbil. Thanks for stopping by."

A woman walks in with her pet tucked under her arm.

"I don't work on sewer rats," I quickly explain.

"This is a Chihuahua," she says, offended.

"Sorry. How can I help you?"

"Our neighbors have a ferocious German shepherd who's giving little Buffy here a nervous disorder. The big bully continually attacks him. In fact, yesterday the shepherd had Buffy in his mouth, shaking him unmercifully. I thought he was going to devour my sweet little poochy. It was practically cannibalism."

"What'd you expect," I ask her. "It's a dog-eat-dog world out there."

"Huh?"

"Will that be cash, check or credit card?"

The Same Old Grind

I'm reading the paper, and the phone rings.

I glance at the caller ID and see that it says "unavailable." Usually, this can only mean three or four things, none of them good, all of them requiring me to spend money.

But it's hard to resist a ringing phone.

"Hello."

"Is this Mr. Borengasser?" a woman's voice inquires.

"Yes," I reply. But I'm getting an uneasy feeling.

"This is Dr. Thistle's office."

Uh-oh.

"To whom do you wish to speak?" I ask, using a Guatemalan accent. "This is Dexter Grasscrosser."

"Too late, Mr. Borengasser," she says. "I recognize your voice. I'm calling to remind you of your dental appointment tomorrow."

"That's impossible," I assert. "I was just there last week. Who is this really?"

"It's been six months."

"Six months? I can't be six months older. I just looked in the mirror this morning. Are you sure?"

"I'm sure. We'll see you at 8:30 AM tomorrow morning."

"Ah … ah … listen, did I mention anything about my hepatitis problem?"

"Sorry, Mr. Borengasser, you used that one last time. Don't forget now. 8:30."

It's 9:15 AM.

I'm at the dentist's office, sprawled out in that special chair that only Dr. Frankenstein could love. My teeth have already been cleaned and examined. But I've got one cavity that they want to fix today. Dr. Thistle drops by for a little pre-torture repartee.

"Good morning," he smiles. "I understand you weren't too excited about coming to see us."

"Nurse Sadisto tricked me," I pout.

"Well, last time, when she left a message with your wife, you never showed up."

"Dental appointments are like subpoenas," I explain. "They're invalid unless delivered directly to the correct person."

"We're only trying to keep your teeth healthy," he says.

"It's nothing personal, Doc, but when I want to put something in my mouth, it's usually something on the order of a cheeseburger, not two or three hands, a metal pick and a small vacuum cleaner. Besides, the last dentist I went to used to work on my teeth with a jackhammer. It left psychological scars—come to think of it, physical scars, too."

"Have you ever tried gas?" he asks.

"What kind—nerve or mustard?"

"No, no," he explains, "this is gas that works as a painkiller."

"Hey, I'll try anything."

Ten minutes later, I'm frolicking on a hillside with Bambi, Thumper and Flower. I hear something in the distance and ask my new friends, "What's that faraway noise? It sounds like a dentist drill."

"Oh, no," replies Thumper. "That's just Boxley the Bear. He's grouchy this morning."

"What do you want to do next?" asks Bambi.

I consider the question. "I don't know," I finally respond. "Why don't we go swimming in that babbling brook, and then sing some show tunes?"

They love the idea.

The next thing I know, I'm staring up at Dr. Thistle.

"We're all done," he says.

"Done? Are you serious?"

"How was the gas?"

"Not bad."

"Good," he says. "So, we'll see you again for your next checkup?"

"Sure. How about tomorrow?"

The Plumber

I WALK over to the phone.

"I'm going to call the plumber," I announce.

"Why?" asks the lovely Mrs. Borengasser. "There's nothing wrong."

"I know, but he's always so late that I'm sure something'll be busted by the time he gets here."

She nods, understanding perfectly.

I remember the last time I phoned the plumber.

"What's the problem?" the plumber asks.

"An emergency!" I blurt out into the telephone receiver. "A busted water pipe in the basement!"

I immediately realize that I've made a serious tactical blunder. You must never use the word "emergency" to a plumber. Everything is an emergency to a plumber. You don't call and invite him to stop by and flush your toilet a few times. No, you only call when the commode is erupting like Mount Helena. Besides, plumbers have heard the word "emergency" so often it's lost its meaning.

I quickly try to repair the damage. "It's a matter of life and death!" I shriek, forcing my voice up a couple of octaves.

I hear him stifle a yawn. I figure I must be getting through to him or he wouldn't have bothered to stifle it.

"A gang of grandmothers are trapped down there," I improvise. "And ... and ... puppies. Dozens of puppies. Oh, yeah, and four football tickets that I'm trying to give away. Fifty-yard line." I wait, scarcely daring to breathe.

"We'll get over as soon as we can," he finally says.

Doom. This is the worst possible thing he can say. In PlumberSpeak, "getting there as soon as I can" means "Sorry, pal, I'm busy. I'll see you when I see you."

He shows up three days later. Of course, by then we have so much water in the basement that I've had it stocked with bluegill and smallmouth bass, and we're sponsoring a fishing derby for the United Way.

It was then that I decide that the only way to get a plumber to my house on time is to call him before I actually have a problem.

The lovely Mrs. Borengasser speaks up before I finish dialing. "Isn't there some other way to get a plumber when we need him besides calling him when we don't?"

I set the receiver down. I consider the problem. And I come up with an idea. "Do you recall the old theory that talking to your plants makes them healthier?" I ask.

"Ahh ... yes," she says cautiously.

"Well, perhaps the same kind of thing would work with our appliances and plumbing fixtures," I suggest.

"Please," she entreats. "I beg of you. Don't tell me you want to chat with the toilet."

"Now, think about it. We take our appliances and plumbing for granted. Maybe a garbage disposal is just like anyone else—it needs love. Maybe it wouldn't break down so often if it thought we cared. Maybe if we just gave our appliances names, it would make for a cheerier work environment for them. In fact, we already call the toilet 'John.' So we're off to a good start. What do you think?"

"I think you should go ahead and call the plumber."

Later that night, I'm tucking in young Pete, our son. I have an inspiration. "Why don't you become a plumber when you grow up," I suggest.

"I don't want to become a plumber, Dad."

"Then marry one," I tell him.

Suddenly, I remember something. "And, by the way, try to stop up the toilet. The plumber will be here the day after tomorrow."

Shoes

THE SUBJECT is shoes.

I have them. You have them. Your horse has them.

Maybe you don't think of shoes often. Or perhaps you're obsessed with them, which once meant that either you had a foot fetish or you were Imelda Marcos.

Over the years, there has been a growing worldwide fascination with shoes. The popularity of shoe museums, shoe exhibits, books on shoes and auctions of celebrity shoes seems to support this claim. One shoe scholar even said that mankind always becomes more preoccupied with shoes at the end of the millennium. (I knew she was a shoe scholar because of all the footnotes.)

I must be out of touch. I haven't caught myself daydreaming about shoes lately. I've never been to a shoe museum. (And I've instructed the lovely Mrs. Borengasser, that if I ever express an interest in visiting one, to shoot me.) I may have accidentally been exposed to a shoe exhibit at one time or another, but I've repressed the memory. I haven't read a book on shoes. I've never purchased a celebrity shoe.

I'm not sure I understand this phenomenon. Shoes cover feet. Feet are unattractive. Feet have bunions, corns, blisters, fungus, ingrown toenails and even disfigured toes. (I myself have toes that only Quasimodo could love.) Feet can be flat and have fallen arches. Feet are mostly used to move your head from one place to another. Consequently, it seems misguided to glamorize something so closely associated with feet.

Shoes also protect feet. Sometimes the only thing between you and a wad of chewing gum, or you and the foulest, nastiest pile of goop you can imagine, is your shoe. And while you may admire the job that shoes perform, this is not exactly the stuff of romantic charm.

To find out if you're shoe-challenged, here's a short quiz to see if you're up on your shoe lore.

1. We'll begin with the basics. A shoe is ...
    a. an item of footwear;
    b. a newspaper cartoon character;
    c. a type of fly used in pies.
2. Doctor Scholl was ...
    a. the creator of an exercise sandal;
    b. Elvis's podiatrist;
    c. the business partner of Doc Marten.
3. Hush Puppy is ...
    a. a shoe with a silly name;
    b. a fried cornmeal ball;
    c. what you yell at your new dog at three in

the morning.

4. Complete this sentence; "If the shoe fits …"

   a. wear it;

   b. buy it;

   c. eat it.

5. A last is …

   a. a foot-like form used to make and repair shoes;

   b. the opposite of a first;

   c. the straw that camels hate.

6. If your lace becomes tangled around the flap of your shoe, you are …

   a. inept;

   b. going to trip;

   c. tongue-tied.

7. Birkenstocks are …

   a. trendy sandals;

   b. shares of the Birken Corporation

   c. the way lawbreaking Birkens are punished.

8. A cobbler is …

   a. a sole man;

   b. a fruity dessert;

   c. a shoddy individual.

If you chose answer "a" on each of the above questions, you get a perfect score. If you picked nothing but "b's" or "c's," you don't know shoes from Shinola.

But don't worry. It's not a permanent condition. You can still learn all about shoes.

And just to get you started, here's a bit of wisdom I've picked up over the years that I'm willing to share: even though shoes seem to be available in a tremendous variety of sizes, this is actually an optical illusion. Every shoe is only one foot long.

The Personals

IF YOU'VE GOTTEN to the point where you're disappointed in every person you meet, if every relationship turns out to be a disaster, I've got great news for you. I've discovered a source of people with no problems, no hang-ups, not even zits.

I found a group of them listed on the Internet under the heading of "personals." And since then, I've even seen some of these miraculous folks described in print publications.

I was amazed. These people were flawless. Perfect. Not a hair out of place. They were all attractive, athletic, intelligent, honest, sensitive, sincere and outgoing. They loved the outdoors, movies and reading. Most of them were ISO a LTR, which means "in search of" a "long-term relationship." There were SWFs (single white females) and DBMs (divorced black males) and WHCPFs (widowed Hispanic Christian professional females).

Of course, I was already familiar with the personals and had even glanced at one or two over the years. But until I sat down and read several dozen of them, I had no idea that these individuals were all so extraordinary.

I had never imagined anyone like these folks. Most of the people I know lose their tempers over insignificant matters, belch when they think they're alone, get depressed occasionally, are somewhat dissatisfied with their station in life and need to lose a pound or two. I begin thinking how wonderful it would be to have a few exemplary friends like the ones in the personals.

Miraculously, I found that for just a few dollars, I could actually make contact with some of them and maybe even meet one or two of these paragons of humanity. I decide to set up a few meetings. Since I already have an LTR with the lovely Mrs. Borengasser, I'm obviously only ISO a few interesting people as acquaintances.

Potential New Friend #1: Bob, an SWM. I agree to meet Bob in a coffee shop, but when I arrive, I can't locate him. Finally, a small, pale, squatty man comes over and introduces himself as Bob.

I'm confused. "Aren't you supposed to be tall, swarthy and athletic?" I ask.

"Hey, are looks that important to you?" he demands shrilly. "Are you that shallow?"

"And aren't you supposed to be pleasant and easygoing?"

"Oh, yeah. Sure," he stammers. "Easygoing. But

enough about me. Tell me about yourself."

"Well, I'm scouting for an interesting guy who, along with a wife or girlfriend, might, from time to time, go out to eat and maybe catch a movie with me and the lovely Mrs. Borengasser."

Bob stares at me in disbelief and then proceeds to berate me for wasting his time.

"Excuse me," I finally interrupt, perplexed, "but aren't you supposed to be sensitive and understanding?"

He doesn't even say goodbye.

Potential New Friend #2: Caroline, a DWF. Not wishing to duplicate my previous mistakes, I tell Caroline right off the bat that I'm not interested in an LTR. She says fine and we agree to meet in a bookstore. So far, so good.

I'm a little nervous, though, because Caroline has descried herself as "full-figured and attractive," and I wouldn't want someone to get the wrong idea. No problem. She actually resembles the jut-jawed Queen of Hearts in *Alice in Wonderland*.

"The ad said you have a good sense of humor," I mention.

"I sure do," she admits, and tells me a joke so raunchy it'd make a porn star blush. She laughs so hard that she snorts out a fine spray of her cappuccino.

I quickly tell her that the lovely Mrs. Borengasser and I are looking for an interesting couple with whom to socialize, and I ask her if she has a boyfriend or fiancé who might want to go along.

She is outraged. "What kind of person do you think I am?"

I have to admit that's a really good question.

At first I think my singular lack of success is a personal problem. Perhaps I'm not worthy of these faultless folks. Why should they be interested in me, a mere mortal?

But then a thought occurs to me. Maybe I could use the personals to find compatible companions, not by contacting those who are already listed, but by placing my own ad. I quickly dash off my own personal personal, "MWM, who's mostly cheerful but has terrible semiannual funk, is somewhat stubborn, keeps a messy desk and likes double crostics, overeating and otters, ISO someone who thinks that, though far from perfect, this MWM may not be all that bad."

Spring

AHH ... SPRING.

For most people their favorite season.

But there are many different interpretations of spring—when it begins and when it ends. It all depends on who and where you are.

For instance, if you're a meteorologist, spring officially begins on March 20th, the vernal equinox, the day the sun crosses the equator on its way back up to the Northern Hemisphere. This is, of course, utterly ridiculous, because, on March 20th, many areas of the country are in the middle of a blizzard. So what kind of spring is that?

If you're a male robin, spring starts when a female robin sidles up to you and tweets, "Hey, big boy. Nice plumage." Then, in a dramatic replay of the age-old courting ritual between males and females of all species, the female robin will want to discuss the nest and the relationship, and the male will simply want to peck the eyes out of the other rival robins.

If you're a bee, spring kicks in with your first intoxicating snort of pollen.

If you're a young man, according to the poet Tennyson, spring begins when your "fancy lightly turns to thoughts of love." (For further explanation, see above birds and bees.)

If you're a Wal-Mart employee, spring arrives when there are at least two cash registers open in the Lawn and Garden Department.

If you're a groundhog from Punxsutawney, Pennsylvania, you don't have a clue. Spring begins when the Punxsutawney mayor says it does.

If you're a Major League Baseball manager, spring starts when you kick dirt on the first umpire of the season.

For many people, spring is a matter of geography.

If you live in northern Minnesota, spring begins on July 15th and, unfortunately, ends a day and a half later.

If you live in Key West, spring isn't even a season. It's a kind of water.

If you live in Antarctica, spring is a totally alien concept. You've heard wild tales of something called "spring," but you really don't know much about it. The richest man in town supposedly has a photo of flowers growing in a snowless garden. But you know that's impossible. The picture's obviously been doctored.

There are other possible signs of spring.

For some, spring begins when you plant your second batch of tomatoes of the year. (The first batch always brings on the last killer frost.)

For others, spring commences when you take the mower out for the first grass cutting of the season and discover that you left gas in the tank, which ruined the carburetor.

For still others, spring gets under way when you first try on your swimsuit and realize you can't get into it without a vat of petroleum jelly and a crow bar.

Spring can also get going with the annual house cleaning, when you'll find dust balls the size of shrubs.

Some mark spring from the first flea infestation.

Perhaps, for most people, spring is mainly an attitude, a time for looking forward to more forgiving times and cheerier weather.

But for me, spring has nothing to do with the fact that March 20th was officially the first day of spring. Or that the professional ice hockey season is almost over for the year.

As far as I'm concerned, there is only one sure sign of spring, indisputable and absolute.

And it happened today.

I went to the mailbox and discovered that I'd just received the year's first Christmas catalog.

Spring is here.

Apologies

PUBLIC APOLOGIES have been in vogue for years. Heads of state apologize for events of the past, some that occurred decades or even centuries ago. Celebrities apologize for their latest outrageous behavior. A psycho killer can get a reduced sentence if he or she apologizes to the victim's family in court.

Now, I like a good apology as well as the next guy. There's something wonderful about having someone say, "Sorry. I was wrong." But I've also noticed that when people apologize, they often think that gets them off the hook. No other action is necessary. This is obviously not the case or there'd be no such thing as attorneys.

An apology is supposed to be good for the soul. Unfortunately, they don't say whose soul. A lot depends on whether you're the apologizer or the apologizee. If someone is telling me he's sorry for being a first-class jerk, fine. But being a jerk is not something I ever want to admit. So, even though apologizing is trendy, I'm not certain I'm ready to follow the crowd.

But then I realize that, as a member of the human race, the family of man, I'm related to every person who has gone before and all those who will follow after. I have a share in all of mankind's accomplishments, past, present and future, whether it's Neil Armstrong's moon walk or Earl Mitchell's moon pie.

I'm always quick to accept praise. Suppose someone says to me, "Hey, aren't you a member of the human race, the same species as Shakespeare, the Queen Mum and the Three Stooges, the life form who developed computers, zippers and aerosol string?"

I immediately respond with a fair amount of arrogance, "Yeah, that's me, all right. We also developed space flight, Key lime pie and Donald Duck. What has your measly, two-bit species done lately?"

Nevertheless, if I'm willing to take credit for the good, I also must accept responsibility for the bad. Humanity's triumphs are my triumphs, but, unfortunately, its mistakes are mine as well. For every Mother Teresa, there's a Stormtrooper Teresa.

So to clear the air, please—all of you out there—accept my sincere and heartfelt apologies for:

The sacking of Rome

Gangsta rap

Cutting you off during rush hour and then running that red light

The French Revolution

Attorneys

Going through the supermarket express
 checkout with more than ten items

Chewing tobacco and spit cups

Custer's Last Stand

Sodom and Gomorrah

Your bad luck with relationships

The Black Plague (and all the other colored
 plagues)

Men

Women

Children

Vanity plates

Professional wrestling

Communism

Capitalism

Reality TV

Airport security

Spam (computer, not the canned delicacy)

Witchcraft

The general unfairness of life

Weenie dogs

Heredity

Your lousy job

Ivan the Terrible and Vlad the Impaler

The Ice Age

The Stone Age

Your age

Republicans

Democrats
Jack the Ripper
The Great Flood
The Great Wall of China
The Great Vowel Shift
The Titanic
Your thankless, no account kids
Pickled beets
Okra
The future.

Wow, I'm amazed. That was remarkably easy. And my soul and I suddenly feel great. Refreshed. Even better, now that I've apologized, I'm completely blameless for these evils.

Glancing over this list, however, I realize I've left out many, many other atrocities for which I could have apologized, such as synchronized swimming and North Korea.

But I ask you, Mr. or Ms. Goody Two-Shoes, are you so darned faultless? Not hardly. You're as much to blame for the human condition as I am. Would it hurt you, for once in your life, to say you're sorry for World War II, head lice and the Potato Famine? Take a little responsibility, for goodness' sake. Come on. Apologize to the rest of us.

And, by the way, if you're offended by this column, tough braunschweiger. So I'm sorry already.

Mo Mo, We Hardly Knew Ye

"**Quick! Come, look,**" calls the lovely Mrs. Borengasser. "Molly's having her puppies."

"Puppies! Good lord! I don't know nothing about birthing puppies!" I shriek like Prissy in *Gone with the Wind*. "Do we call the vet, 911 or a midwife? I'll boil some water. They always boil water."

"I'm sure Molly will know what to do," she assures me.

And, eight puppies later, I find she's right.

What a mess of mutts. There's rambunctious Waggedy Ann and narcoleptic Brownie and big, bad Buster and bigger, badder Butch and Snow White and Calvin and Venus.

And then there's Mort, white and brown and black with a brown eye patch.

That was a long time ago.

Over the years, we have had many names for Mort. We called him Mo Mo because he was such a cute pup. By comparison, Helen of Troy was homely as a mud fence.

We called him Mortimer because he was intelligent and dignified. In fact, he was smart enough to join Mensa but didn't because he thought it would be pretentious.

We called him Mort the Snort because he would sniff a scent intently and then suddenly exhale loudly. It must have been something like a wine connoisseur cleansing his palette between tastings.

We called him The Perfect Master because of his mystical Zen-like approach to life. At one time, we even decided to send him to divinity school.

Mort was a dog of many talents. He could catch popcorn in his mouth. If you think that's easy, try doing it with no hands.

Mort understood the art of fishing, and would get incredibly excited when he saw the bobber go down. We'd pull the fish in, Mort would lick it, and we'd toss it back in the water. I suppose you could call it a Kiss and Release Program. A cynic might say that Mort simply had a taste for sushi, but we knew he blessed all creatures great and small. (Except, of course, for the vile squirrel.)

Mort was a canine of letters, having made a cameo appearance in a romantic novel. He never let this go to his head.

Mort was an escape artist, a backyard Houdini. He, Molly and Sasha would defy all efforts to keep them fenced in. Once he was gone for a week. We thought he was gone for good, but then one night, he appeared on the porch, starving and barely able to walk. A German shepherd—the Good Shepherd, as we always later referred to him—had led Mort back and wouldn't leave till he knew Mort was in safe hands.

It turned out that Mort had been hit by a car or truck, and his hip was severely fractured. He was on the operating table for hours, and ended up with more metal in him than a '55 Chevy.

But he recuperated quickly, and, except for a slight hitch in his get-along, you'd never suspect that he'd almost bought the kennel.

In his old age—as old men do—he became grumpy, cantankerous and incontinent.

The metal in his hips eventually caught up with him. Day after day, he would limp in a slow, agonizing path around the yard because he knew what would happen the day he stopped.

But stop he did.

We think of Mort often.

He was a fine friend and a devoted companion.

He never made it to divinity school.

Printed in the United States
201871BV00001B/1-150/P

9 780979 520419